Equinox
*a poem meditation by*
Desiray Idowes

Copyright © Desiray Howes
Poem: "Equinox" May 2017

All Rights Reserved
including the right of reproduction of this book,
copying, or storage in any form or means, including
electronic,without prior written permission of the author.

ISBN: 978-1-946088-04-8

1.Poetry 2.Nature 3.Seasons 4.Title

Matrika Press
164 Lancey Street
Pittsfield, Maine 04967
(760) 889-5428

Editor@MatrikaPress.com

www.MatrikaPress.com

First Edition

Printed in the USA

Cover Art by: Desiray Howes

Cover and Interior Design by: "Twinkle" Marie Manning

# Poet's Dedication

To my family and friends who
believed in me when I didn't.

Equinox

My favorite time of the year is when winter clashes with spring.

When night falls

and winter takes its last stand,

and in the morning

spring breaks

winter's grass on the land.

*Winter but a shadow*

on the face of the Earth.

When the moon

and the sun

battle for the morning sky.

Exchanging quiet words

as the suns rays

fill the surrounding area.

The moments when

the veil between earth

and the universe

is nearly transgarent.

The colorful sky

distracting us from
the glamour of daylight.

Blocking out our view

of the void above.

My favorite time of the year

is when spring and winter meet,

the melting snow
reviving the life it once took.

*The point where death
and rebirth cross paths*

acknowledging that without one
the other would not exist.

Winter's mark nothing but a thin
blanket upon the Earth's skin.

Plant life delicately rises

from coldness

as it reaches for

the warmth of the sun

as the suns rays
wrag its arms lovingly around it.

Birds begin singing
for their return home.

A perfectly balanced melody

carried by the wind.

My favorite time of the year

is when the snow tenderly
kisses the earth goodbye

*lingering*

for a short period of time.

My favorite time of the year

is when spring

meets winter

and greets it with open arms,

coinciding for but a moment

before the two gass

waiting anxiously

to meet again.

# Equinox
*by Desiray Howes*

My favorite time of the year is when winter clashes with spring. When night falls and winter takes its last stand, and in the morning spring breaks winter's grasp on the land. Winter but a shadow on the face of the Earth. When the moon and the sun battle for the morning sky. Exchanging quiet words as the suns rays fill the surrounding area. The moments when the veil between earth and the universe is nearly transparent. The colorful sky distracting us from the glamour of daylight. Blocking out our view of the void above. My favorite time of the year is when spring and winter meet, the melting snow reviving the life it once took. The point where death and rebirth cross paths acknowledging that without one the other would not exist. Winter's mark nothing but a thin blanket upon the Earth's skin. Plant life delicately rises from coldness as it reaches for the warmth of the sun as the suns rays wrap its arms lovingly around it. Birds begin singing for their return home. A perfectly balanced melody carried by the wind. My favorite time of the year is when the snow tenderly kisses the earth goodbye lingering for a short period of time. My favorite time of the year is when spring meets winter and greets it with open arms, coinciding for but a moment before the two pass waiting anxiously to meet again.

Desiray Howes is an emerging poet and artist, from Athens, Maine. As a senior at MCI she made it her goal to really push her creative side, and in doing so made creativity the soul purpose of her senior project. She included this Pocketful book in her final presentation where she shows her creative process, from the inspiration to the obstacles, all the way through to completion. She shares the inner workings of her mind. With the intent to make an impact on the minds of her readers, this is but the first step in her journey.

www.MatrikaPress.com/Desiray-Howes

**Matrika Press** is an independent publishing house dedicated to publishing works in alignment with Unitarian Universalist values and principles.
Its fiscal sponsor is UU Women and Religion: uuwr.org
Matrika Press derives its name from the 50 letters of the Sanskrit alphabet called "the mothers" aka "Matrika."
Kali Ma used the letters to form words, and from the words formed all things...as with the Bible: *"in the beginning was the Word."* People of all backgrounds and faiths agree: *Words are powerful.* More than that: *Their vibrations are creative forces; they bring all things into being.*

www.MatrikaPress.com

# AVAILABLE NOW FROM MATRIKA PRESS

This book is a compilation of women sojourners, sages, mystics, witches, shaman, medicine women, ministers, philosophers, therapists, life coaches, yogis, and more. Their journeys. Their stories. Their teachings and practices. Essays, Poetry, Art, Rituals and Prayers. This anthology is full of useful tools and powerful messages for everyone who is on a spiritual journey to embrace and enjoy. Beloved Contributors include:

- *Anna Huckabee Tull • Bernadette Rombough • Deb Elbaum*
- *Deborah Diamond • Debra Wilson Guttas • Grace Ventura*
- *Janeen Barnett • JoAnne Bassett • Judy Ann Foster*
- *Julie Matheson • Kate Early • Kate Kavanagh • Katherine Glass*
- *Kris Oster • Lea M. Hill • Meghan Gilroy • Morwen Two Feathers*
- *Rustie MacDonald • Shamanaca • Sharon Hinckley • Shawna Allard*
- *Shiloh Sophia • Susan Feathers • Tiffany Cano • Tory Londergan*
- *"Twinkle" Marie Manning • Tziporah Kingsbury • Valerie Sorrentino*

www.MatrikaPress.com

# Seventh Principle Studies & First Source Explorations

    The Seventh UU Principle is: *"Respect for the interdependent web of all existence of which we are a part."*

    The First Source UUs draw faith from is: *"Direct experience of that transcending mystery and wonder, affirmed in all cultures, which moves us to a renewal of the spirit and an openness to the forces which create and uphold life."*

    Evidence to support such is found within the pages of ***The Way of Power***.

www.MatrikaPress.com

## ***Where the Sky has No Stars***

A poetry anthology by Wesley Burton

Wesley's contemplative and imaginative poetry entices readers to face moments of transition. His words explore the inner depths of the psyche, the healing power of nature, and the soul's resilience to move forward out of darkness.

http://MatrikaPress.com/wesley-burton/

www.MatrikaPress.com

# RECOMMENDED SELECTIONS FROM SKINNER HOUSE

### Reaching for the Sun
Rev. Angela Herrera's book of meditations, prayers and invocations provide inspiration to readers and serve as a resource to those seeking powerful liturgical words, grounded in the experiences of everyday life.

### Evening Tide
This book of mediations by Elizabeth Tarbox helps readers to face the darker moments of life, the challenging circumstances that call us to live more fully even when we feel our most empty.

### Stirring the Nation's Heart: Eighteen Stories of Prophetic Unitarians and Universalists of the 19th Century by Polly Peterson
Eighteen compelling stories from the lives of some of the nineteenth-century Transcendentalists and reformers who played key roles in Unitarian Universalist history.

http://www.uua.org/publications/skinnerhouse

# RECOMMENDED SELECTIONS FROM BEACON PRESS

### Claiming the Spirit Within
This wonderful book, edited by Rev. Marilyn Sewell, is a beautiful sourcebook of poetry and prose. A rich and diverse anthology dedicated to the praise of life, it presents the sacredness that emerges when women immerse fully in living lives of spirit while embracing the physical. More than 300 poems celebrating all aspects of women's lives.

http://www.beacon.org/

www.ingramcontent.com/pod-product-compliance
Lightning Source LLC
Chambersburg PA
CBHW071727020426
42333CB00017B/2426